© 2023. Published by Pillar Box Red Publishing Limited. Printed in the EU.

ISBN: 978-1-914536-89-2

Images © Getty Images

Written by Jared Tinslay | Designed by Darryl Tooth

THE
ULTIMATE GUIDE TO THE
PREMIER LEAGUE
2024

CONTENTS

2022-23 SEASON REVIEW

WE LOOK BACK AT THE 2022-23 PREMIER LEAGUE CAMPAIGN MONTH BY MONTH, CHECKING OUT THE BIGGEST MOMENTS AND CHRONICLING THE TITLE RACE...

AUGUST

MEGA MOMENTS!

First goal of the season

Arsenal and Crystal Palace got the new season started under Friday-night floodlights at Selhurst Park, with Gabriel Martinelli scoring the first goal of the 2022-23 campaign! A late Marc Guehi own goal sealed a 2-0 victory for The Gunners in this London Derby!

Stunned at Brentford

Erik ten Hag's reign at Man. United began with a shaky opening-day defeat at home to Brighton but things got even worse at the Brentford Community Stadium – a 4-0 thrashing saw The Red Devils lose their first two games of a season for the first time since 1992-93!

There were handbags on the touchline in Tottenham's dramatic draw with Chelsea at Stamford Bridge! After Harry Kane's late 96th-minute equaliser, Thomas Tuchel and Antonio Conte were sent off after squaring up to each other and almost sparking a full-on brawl!

Head-to-head

St. James' Park thriller

Reigning Prem champions Man. City produced a breathtaking turnaround as they came from 3-1 down to draw at Newcastle in an end-to-end match featuring six goals and an overturned red card! Before th City had won 27 of their previous 28 games when scoring first, so it was still a great result for The Mapgies!

DID YOU KNOW?

Liverpool equalled the biggest win in Premier League history by thrashing newly promoted Bournemouth 9-0 at Anfield!

END OF MONTH TOP FOUR			
	P	Pts	GD
ARSENAL	5	15	+9
MAN. CITY	5	13	+14
TOTTENHAM	5	11	+6
BRIGHTON	5	10	+10

SEPTEMBER
MEGA MOMENTS!

Debut goal

The 2022 summer transfer window slammed shut on September 1 after the biggest deadline day signing in Premier League history: Man. United's £82 million deal for Brazilian trickster Antony from Ajax! Then, three days later, he scored on his debut v Arsenal!

City Ground classic

After Scott Parker was dismissed following Bournemouth's Liverpool humiliation, The Cherries overturned a two-goal deficit to win 3-2 against Nottingham Forest at the City Ground, giving Gary O'Neil his first win as interim boss in one of the games of the season!

New Chelsea boss

Following the sacking of Thomas Tuchel, Chelsea hired Brighton's Graham Potter as their new manager early in September, with The Seagulls replacing him with former Shakhtar Donetsk and Sassuolo gaffer Roberto de Zerbi just over a week later!

Royal tribute

On September 9, all Premier League matches scheduled for September 10-12 were postponed as a mark of respect after the death of Queen Elizabeth II, with the following games paying tribute to the late monarch.

DID YOU KNOW?
Heung-Min Son became the first Tottenham player to score a PL hat-trick as a sub in the game against Leicester, netting three times in just over 14 minutes!

END OF MONTH TOP FOUR

	P	Pts	GD
ARSENAL	7	18	+10
MAN. CITY	7	17	+17
TOTTENHAM	7	17	+11
BRIGHTON	6	13	+6

OCTOBER
MEGA MOMENTS!

Hat-trick heroes

Phil Foden and Erling Haaland both scored hat-tricks as Man. City dished out a 6-3 derby day thrashing to Man. United at the Etihad at the start of the month. It would have been even more humiliating for The Red Devils without Anthony Martial's two late consolation goals!

Three second-half goals, ending with a stoppage time strike by Rodrigo Bentancur, completed a stunning comeback by Tottenham as they fought from two goals down to beat Bournemouth 3-2 at the Vitality Park!

Late drama

Seagulls' revenge

Graham Potter's first game as Chelsea boss was a nightmare as he lost 4-1 to his old club Brighton, with jubilant Seagulls supporters chanting, "you're getting sacked in the morning" at their former gaffer!

Arsenal ended the month with a thumping 5-0 win at home to Nottingham Forest, thanks to two goals from super sub Reiss Nelson - his first Premier League strikes since 2020!

Banging brace

DID YOU KNOW?
Leandro Trossard became the first-ever Brighton player to score a Premier League hat-trick in The Seagulls' thrilling 3-3 draw with Liverpool!

END OF MONTH TOP FOUR

	P	Pts	GD
ARSENAL	12	31	+19
MAN. CITY	12	29	+26
TOTTENHAM	13	26	+10
NEWCASTLE	13	24	+14

NOVEMBER
MEGA MOMENTS!

Gross' late winner

Pascal Gross' late goal earned on form Brighton a dramatic 3-2 win over Wolves in a thrilling game at Molineux that featured four first-half goals and a red card to the hosts' right-back Nelson Semedo!

Elland Road explodes

Crysencio Summerville was the match-winner for Leeds as they came from 3-1 down to beat Bournemouth 4-3 in a Premier League classic at Elland Road! The winger calmly slotted the ball beyond Mark Travers in the 84th-minute to seal a memorable victory for Jesse Marsch's side!

A week later, Leeds were involved in another bonkers PL game, but this time they were on the other end of the scoreline! Rodrigo Bentancur scored twice in the final ten minutes to snatch an incredible 4-3 victory for Tottenham, despite trailing three times!

Bentancur brace

Talented teen

In the final Premier League game before the 2022 World Cup, Man. United teenager Alejandro Garnacho came off the bench to score his first-ever Premier League goal in the third minute of stoppage time to clinch a 2-1 victory over Fulham!

DID YOU KNOW?
Unai Emery's first game in charge of Aston Villa ended The Villans' 27-year wait for a home win over Man. United in the Premier League!

END OF MONTH TOP FOUR

	P	Pts	GD
ARSENAL	14	37	+22
MAN. CITY	14	32	+26
NEWCASTLE	15	30	+18
TOTTENHAM	15	29	+10

DECEMBER
MEGA MOMENTS!

Christmas cards

Christmas Day had passed but there were some late cards being brandished on Boxing Day as football returned after the World Cup; Crystal Palace duo Tyrick Mitchell and James Tomkins both saw red in The Eagles' 3-0 defeat at home to Fulham!

Erling Haaland, who was born in Leeds when his father Alfe-Inge played for The Whites, marked his return to Yorkshire by scoring twice at Elland Road to become the fastest player to reach 20 PL goals!

20th goal in 14th game

OG nightmare

Leicester centre-back Wout Faes became only the fourth player to score two own goals in a Premier League game in The Foxes' 2-1 loss to Liverpool, as they threw away an early lead at Anfield!

At just 18 years old, Irish wonderkid Evan Ferguson became Brighton's youngest Premier League scorer of all time, and the youngest-ever Irishman to score in the Prem, in the 4-2 defeat to Arsenal on New Year's Eve!

Record-breaker

DID YOU KNOW?
In Southampton's 2-1 loss to Fulham, James Ward-Prowse became the fifth player to score both an own goal and a direct free-kick in the same PL game!

END OF MONTH TOP FOUR

	P	Pts	GD
ARSENAL	16	43	+26
MAN. CITY	16	36	+28
NEWCASTLE	17	34	+21
MAN. UNITED	16	32	+4

JANUARY
MEGA MOMENTS!

Chelsea's Joao Felix became the first player to be sent off on his Premier League debut since 2014, and the first-ever player sent off on his Chelsea debut in the Premier League, in The Blues' 2-1 defeat to Fulham at Craven Cottage!

Disastrous debut

The mega on-form Marcus Rashford kept up his stunning scoring streak since the World Cup to complete an incredible 2-1 comeback win for Man. United over local rivals City at Old Trafford!

Derby delight

Six months after beating them at the Emirates, Arsenal won away against arch-rivals Tottenham to complete the league double over their North London enemies for the first time since 2014, thanks to Hugo Lloris' own goal and a Martin Odegaard screamer!

Double trouble

Excellent Eddie

A week later Arsenal beat another huge rival, as Eddie Nketiah's last-minute goal gave them a 3-2 win over Man. United to restore their five-point advantage over closest title rivals Man. City going into February!

DID YOU KNOW?
Erling Haaland's hat-trick v Wolves took him to 18 goals from 11 Premier League home games – a new City record in a single season!

END OF MONTH TOP FOUR	P	Pts	GD
ARSENAL	19	50	+29
MAN. CITY	20	45	+33
NEWCASTLE	20	39	+22
MAN. UNITED	20	39	+1

FEBRUARY
MEGA MOMENTS!

Magic Maddison

Struggling Leicester came from behind twice against Aston Villa to win their first Premier League game since November, with the pulsating clash ending 4-2, despite The Villans dominating with 63% possession and 19 shots!

Harry Kane netted his 267th goal for Tottenham to overtake Jimmy Greaves as the club's top goalscorer! The strike came in a crazy 1-0 win over Man. City that ended with a late red card for Spurs' Cristian Romero!

Spurs legend

Sacked

Southampton parted company with Nathan Jones just three months and 14 games into his first managerial position at a Premier League club! The former Luton boss had taken over from Ralph Hasenhuttl in November!

It was billed as a must-watch top-of-the-table showdown, and Arsenal v Man. City delivered the goods! The visitors left London with three points after goals from Kevin De Bruyne, Jack Grealish and Erling Haaland cancelled out Bukayo Saka's penalty!

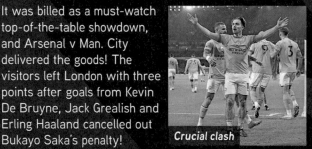
Crucial clash

DID YOU KNOW?
Chelsea's deal for Argentina midfielder Enzo Fernandez from Benfica for a British record fee of £106 million was completed on February 1!

END OF MONTH TOP FOUR	P	Pts	GD
ARSENAL	24	57	+29
MAN. CITY	25	55	+39
MAN. UNITED	24	49	+13
TOTTENHAM	25	45	+1

MARCH

MEGA MOMENTS!

Dramatic scenes

Tottenham were winning 3-1 against Southampton with 13 minutes of the game left, when Theo Walcott sparked The Saints' comeback! James Ward-Prowse then equalised from the penalty spot in the 93rd minute, with Antonio Conte ranting about his players after the game!

JWP's penalty

Reiss Nelson was Arsenal's hero as his 97th-minute winner sealed an astonishing comeback from 2-0 down to a 3-2 victory against relegation-threatened Bournemouth at the Emirates!

Comeback king

Conte left Tottenham after that crazy clash with Southampton, and that wasn't the league's only managerial change in March. At the age of 75, Roy Hodgson came out of retirement to take over his old club Crystal Palace after Patrick Vieira was sacked!

Liverpool thrashed their rivals Man. United 7-0 at Anfield in one of the biggest Premier League humiliations in history, especially with the score only at 1-0 going into the half-time break! In the process, Mohamed Salah became The Reds' record scorer in the PL!

Anfield legend

DID YOU KNOW?
The 97+ minutes between Philip Billing and Reiss Nelson's goals in March is a PL record for the biggest margin between a game's first and last goals!

END OF MONTH TOP FOUR			
	P	Pts	GD
ARSENAL	28	69	+40
MAN. CITY	27	61	+42
MAN. UNITED	26	50	+6
TOTTENHAM	28	49	+12

APRIL

MEGA MOMENTS!

Meltdown

Arsenal needed two late goals against Southampton to rescue a point against the Premier League's bottom-placed club! More draws followed against West Ham and Liverpool, as the pressure on the leaders really started to ramp up!

Man. City masterclass

Man. City put in one of their best performances of the season in the title showdown with Arsenal! In a devastating De Bruyne display, the Belgium hero scored two goals and assisted another in a comfortable 4-1 victory in front of a jubilant Etihad!

April was a tough month for Tottenham! After losing to stoppage time goals against both Bournemouth and Liverpool, they were later smashed 6-1 at Newcastle, conceding five goals inside the first 21 minutes with Sweden striker Alexander Isak notching a brace!

Brighton scored six goals in a match as a top-flight club for the first time ever in their 6-0 thrashing of Wolves thanks to brilliant braces from each of Deniz Undav, Pascal Gross and Danny Welbeck!

Unstoppable Seagulls

Magpies run riot

DID YOU KNOW?
Leeds set a new Premier League record for goals conceded in a single month during April, shipping 23 goals in seven games!

END OF MONTH TOP FOUR			
	P	Pts	GD
MAN. CITY	32	76	+54
ARSENAL	33	75	+40
NEWCASTLE	33	65	+34
MAN. UNITED	32	63	-10

Yorkshire-born boys

MAY
MEGA MOMENTS!

Safety secured

There were really contrasting scenes at the City Ground, as Taiwo Awoniyi's early goal against Arsenal clinched Nottingham's Forest survival and ended The Gunners' dreams of becoming champions!

Century of goals

With the shackles off, Man. City celebrated their title triumph with a 1-0 win over Chelsea at the Etihad Stadium! The result brought up their 100th home goal of the 2022-23 campaign in all competitions!

Newcastle secured a place in the Champions League for the first time since 2003 with a 0-0 draw against Leicester - and were joined by Man. United three days later after The Red Devils thrashed Chelsea 4-1!

Back in the big time

Everton ecstasy

It was a dramatic last day of the Premier League at the bottom of the table, with two of Everton, Leeds and Leicester all in danger of going down! The Toffees' 1-0 win over Bournemouth secured their safety, despite The Foxes beating West Ham!

DID YOU KNOW?
Arsenal led the Premier League table for 248 days in the 2022-23 season, the most for a team who failed to win the title in English top-flight history!

END OF MONTH TOP FOUR			
	P	Pts	GD
MAN. CITY	38	89	+61
ARSENAL	38	84	+45
MAN. UNITED	38	75	+15
NEWCASTLE	38	71	+35

CHAMPIONS

36 Erling Haaland's 36 goals broke the record for the most by one player in a single Premier League season!

62 They averaged 62% ball possession – a Premier League high!

10+ Pep Guardiola became only the fifth manager to win 10+ major honours in charge of English clubs!

16 No player provided more Premier League assists than De Bruyne in 2022-23!

12 Their 12-game winning run was a record high in the 2022-23 PL campaign!

CHAMPIONS 2022/23

CITY!

5

Man. City became the third team to win the English top flight in five out of six seasons!

100

They were the only side in Europe's top five leagues to score 100 goals at home in all competitions!

8

Kevin De Bruyne provided eight PL assists for Haaland in 2022-23, making them the league's deadliest partnership!

89

Their pass success rate of 89% was also the best in the league for the 2022-23 season!

3

They became just the second team to win the Premier League in three straight seasons, after rivals Man. United!

15

PREMIER LEAGUE
PLAYERS OF THE MONTH

THE 2022 WORLD CUP IN THE MIDDLE OF THE CAMPAIGN SAW THE AWARDS FOR NOVEMBER AND DECEMBER COMBINED IN AN UNPRECEDENTED MOVE. AS IT HAPPENED, ONLY THE TOP FOUR TEAMS WERE REPRESENTED IN THE PREMIER LEAGUE PLAYER OF THE MONTH AWARDS.

AUGUST
ERLING HAALAND
MAN. CITY

The Norway net-buster had the perfect start to his Premier League career, scoring a record nine goals in his first five games in the competition! He became only the sixth player to score hat-tricks in consecutive Premier League games - doing so against Crystal Palace and Nottingham Forest - and the first star since Harry Kane in 2017! The legend has done it twice though, so Haaland has another record to chase!

SEPTEMBER
MARCUS RASHFORD
MAN. UNITED

Man. United only played two Premier League games in September but Rashford was directly involved in all four of his side's goals, including a match-winning brace to put an end to Arsenal's unbeaten start to the season. It marked the second PL Player of the Month prize of his career, almost four years after winning his first in January 2019.

OCTOBER
MIGUEL ALMIRON
NEWCASTLE

Nobody scored more goals than Almiron in October, with the Newcastle midfielder netting six goals in six games - including the PL Goal of the Month against Fulham! He became only the second Paraguayan to be named the Player of the Month, after former Blackburn striker Roque Santa Cruz, and the first Magpies player since Joe Willock in May 2021!

NOVEMBER & DECEMBER
MARTIN ODEGAARD
ARSENAL

The Arsenal captain was directly involved in six goals (three goals and three assists) across November and December - more than any other player! He became the first Arsenal player to win the award since Pierre-Emerick Aubameyang in September 2019 and the second Norwegian after Erling Haaland in August.

JANUARY
MARCUS RASHFORD
MAN. UNITED

Magic Marcus started the new year in fine fashion, busting net in three of Man. United's four matches in January – a goal in the 3-0 win over Bournemouth, the late winner in the Manchester derby and a long-range rocket against Arsenal that was also nominated for the Goal of the Month!

FEBRUARY
MARCUS RASHFORD
MAN. UNITED

Rashford took his January form straight into February, scoring five goals in four matches as The Red Devils sailed through the month without losing! In winning the award, he equalled the Premier League record for the most Player of the Month prizes in a single season, level with Mo Salah's three in 2017-18!

MARCH
BUKAYO SAKA
ARSENAL

March was an historic month for Saka as he won the Premier League Player of the Month prize for the first time in his career! He scored three goals and provided two assists in four games, and at 21 became the youngest Arsenal player to reach double figures for both goals and assists in a single PL season!

APRIL
ERLING HAALAND
MAN. CITY

In four April games, Haaland scored six goals and created two, but more importantly he delivered when it mattered. The two assists came in the crucial win over Arsenal, and he also scored late on against The Gunners, while his strike against Fulham saw him equal the PL record for goals in a season!

PREMIER

PLAYER
OF THE YEAR

ERLING HAALAND

In what was undoubtedly the best debut Premier League season ever, scoring 36 times to break a 29-year-old record for the most goals in a single PL campaign as well as contributing eight assists, Erling Haaland was the deserved winner of the league's Player of the Year prize. His remarkable total of 44 goal involvements is the joint-highest of all-time, equalling a record set by former Arsenal forward Thierry Henry in the 2002-03 season.

"It has been an incredible first season in the Premier League and lifting the trophy in front of our fans at the Etihad was a very special moment for me," the Norwegian declared. "These awards would not have been possible without my amazing teammates, the manager and all of the staff at the club who help me perform on the pitch."

A Man. City player has now won the trophy for four consecutive seasons, with teammate Kevin De Bruyne collecting it in 2019-20 and 2021-22, either side of Ruben Dias' win in 2020-21.

LEAGUE

"I AM HONOURED TO HAVE BECOME THE FIRST PLAYER TO WIN BOTH AWARDS IN THE SAME SEASON — THANK YOU TO EVERYONE WHO VOTED FOR ME."

PLAYERS SHORTLISTED FOR THE AWARD:

ERLING HAALAND
MAN. CITY

MARTIN ODEGAARD
ARSENAL

KEVIN DE BRUYNE
MAN. CITY

BUKAYO SAKA
ARSENAL

HARRY KANE
TOTTENHAM

KIERAN TRIPPIER
NEWCASTLE

MARCUS RASHFORD
MAN. UNITED

YOUNG PLAYER OF THE SEASON

Haaland was also named as the Premier League Young Player of the Season to become the first player to win both awards in the same term. The Young Player of the Season was first awarded in 2019-20 and had been won in both of the last two years by City's Phil Foden, making it a hat-trick for the club.

19

WORDSEARCH

CAN YOU FIND 30 PREMIER LEAGUE MANAGERS – PAST AND PRESENT – IN THE GRID BELOW?

```
Q P Z G U P B G A G E P O S T Y D B K C C I Y R E Y A W I O
Q L W Q F J D G E U O C K Z L W P G D Y C H E T P X N Q Z O
C A R T E T A P A S M K C F Z R C X U I H U Z H Z W E C E J A
P R X R Q V T J X N X D T V F V D W D P V C W S C B E E K Y
C G W Y E D Y X I A E X P Y U G P C N R Z J Q Y Y W L A U E
K N J V Y D B C C W P N G P T N L K D T F M D A P L O G Y I
L I B L V O K M M L J S R O D G E R S C C R P X E W T E M O
P Y I P I V E N D B B B Y Y Q Y S V L G A Y K G E E T C N H
P P E O R Z Y T A W R P U P R E D B N L N C C M R N I Z X F
W A L O S I J X J P S U C V Y W D R L G S N E Q X G B E O T
W R S D O R E Y K J P T C O B C G A W R M A P D I E N O L P
Y D A P X S L A B Y G B M E H W C N W X V O L J A R B P O U
N E R D B B F F P V J Z B M V G O I O W Y F U B V S L Y X L
Q W P E Y G E N L X P C U W S F B E N I T E Z R O R I Q X I
J P O E D E L Y R X I W Y D G K Q R S H U L C K I N L L W S
G G C P H M W R C G S K X M O V W I Q M H T M C M N W A V W
K R H L C O N T E M J P W S K O C V E C Z B B E C H S G A
I Y E K K E P S H K A J J G U A R D I O L A R I U P C O B W
N Q T T B P C K S E Z K C I P Y B J S W Z U K Z M K E Q M
N J T V T T N U C J R C G L Z S X Z E P P V H H D F X Q R A
E E I U E A L M N A N C G G R I M H M Q N Y J O T G O G V N
A K N D R Z O U N C V J T H E G G N Q Y E Y L I D R U T P U
R J O F J E P O X V M W A E B U G P L L Y E O M B G Z I F X
J A B Y F C S B G H E G O C H K V R H Y G D P X T G S H W T
U E T K Q U Z I X N M K H S U J F S E X Q I E M I P B O O F
J R V W G W B O A S E X R C Z P I W V F P O T T E R H O N X
J F X R P S O Z R V R B C G E B U J Q Q Q Z E U B N H I H F
P Y E S A L C P A E Y J H J R X B Y S X R W G W Y I C N O S
L F V W F G U C A K O F Q U C K E G X N S W U W X P E P W K
X B B J V N S E Z W D T C K J E H J V G G L I G M M X F E R
W B U N R Q H K W L B B B B Q Q F E T Y B T V A V E O T K J R O
A K L O P P E D C R M F Y X Z B Y Z B M B Z G Y O C I V H V
```

Allardyce	Bruce	Ferguson	Hughes	Moyes	Ranieri
Ancelotti	Conte	Frank	Kinnear	Pardew	Redknapp
Arteta	Curbishley	Guardiola	Klopp	Pochettino	Rodgers
Benitez	Dyche	Hodgson	Lopetegui	Potter	Silva
Bielsa	Emery	Howe	Mourinho	Pulis	Wenger

STUDY THESE PHOTOS FROM THE 2022-23 PREMIER LEAGUE SEASON AND SEE IF YOU CAN FIND THE TEN DIFFERENCES!

ANSWERS ON PAGE 60

MAN. CITY

2023 POSITION: 1ST

TOP SCORER: ERLING HAALAND (36)
TOP ASSISTS: KEVIN DE BRUYNE (16)
MOST MINUTES: EDERSON (3150)

94
GOALS
A LEAGUE HIGH

33
GOALS CONCEDED
A JOINT-LEAGUE LOW

24
PLAYERS USED - A LEAGUE LOW

In 2023, Man. City joined local rivals United in the history books by completing an amazing hat-trick of Premier League titles, despite being pushed all the way by their closest challengers, Arsenal! The Citizens could go one better in 2023-24 by becoming the first-ever club to lift four PL trophies in a row, which would also be their sixth in seven seasons - another record. With seven PL titles in total, they're the second most successful club in the competition's history, and every win takes them closer to Man. United's all-time record of 13. With Pep Guardiola in charge and Erling Haaland leading the attack, they'll be most people's favourites to win No.8 in 2024 - even if it takes another epic title battle like in the last two seasons!

25,072
PASSES COMPLETED
A LEAGUE HIGH

52
HOME POINTS
A LEAGUE HIGH

9 PENALTIES SCORED
A LEAGUE HIGH

ARSENAL

2023 POSITION: 2ND

TOP SCORER: GABRIEL MARTINELLI & MARTIN ODEGAARD (15)
TOP ASSISTS: BUKAYO SAKA (11)
MOST MINUTES: AARON RAMSDALE (3420)

62
GOALS FROM OPEN PLAY
A JOINT-LEAGUE HIGH

39
AWAY POINTS
A LEAGUE HIGH

1
HOME DEFEAT - A JOINT-LEAGUE LOW

It's hard to believe it now, but it wasn't so long ago that some Arsenal fans wanted #ArtetaOut, which proves how important it is to give a good coach time to work on his team! Nobody expected last season's near-miss after The Gunners finished fifth the season before, and most fans would have been happy with a top four finish, but they'll still feel gutted after spending so much time top of the league. The good news for Arsenal is that they've made loads of brilliant signings over recent years, and their academy is world class, so their squad is packed with exciting young talents who are only going to get better with time. They might have missed out in 2023, but they'll be challenging for trophies again over the next few years!

85%
PASS SUCCESS RATE

24.6
SQUAD'S AVERAGE AGE
A LEAGUE LOW

4 PLAYERS WITH
10+ PL GOALS

MAN. UNITED

2023 POSITION: 3RD

TOP SCORER: MARCUS RASHFORD (17)
TOP ASSISTS: BRUNO FERNANDES & CHRISTIAN ERIKSEN (8)
MOST MINUTES: DAVID DE GEA (3420)

105
THROUGH BALLS
A LEAGUE HIGH

17
CLEAN SHEETS
A LEAGUE HIGH

479
CHANCES
CREATED

10
COUNTER-ATTACK GOALS
A LEAGUE HIGH

119
BRUNO FERNANDES' CHANCES CREATED
A LEAGUE HIGH

There couldn't have been many grumbles from Man. United fans about how last season ended after they managed to re-enter Europe's elite competition and reach two domestic finals in Erik ten Hag's debut season in England! Those achievements shouldn't be taken for granted, especially considering the issues the club had before the Dutch manager's arrival, but now it's time for the club to move forward and look upwards. They're desperate to get their hands on another Premier League trophy to extend their record and they've brought in a calibre of players who should be able to at least help them challenge. Supporters just need to accept that there may be some bumps along the way...

10 HOME GOALS CONCEDED
A LEAGUE LOW

Stats from 2022-23 season

24

NEWCASTLE

2023 POSITION: 4TH

TOP SCORER: CALLUM WILSON (18)
TOP ASSISTS: KIERAN TRIPPIER (7)
MOST MINUTES: KIERAN TRIPPIER (3348)

17
UNBEATEN RUN
A LEAGUE HIGH

3
HOME DEFEATS

14
GOALS FROM OUTSIDE BOX
A LEAGUE HIGH

What a time to be a Newcastle fan! Even with their mega-rich new owners, The Magpies hugely exceeded expectations by finishing in the top four and qualifying for the Champions League so early in this exciting new era for the club - and without even spending huge amounts. They brought out the chequebook in 2023, and more money will be spent in the years to come to make the squad even stronger and fill it with more high-profile players. Of course, spending loads of cash doesn't guarantee success - as Chelsea found out last season - but it feels like only a matter of time before Newcastle end their long wait for a first major domestic trophy since 1955. Could 2023-24 be the season?

33
GOALS CONCEDED
A JOINT-LEAGUE LOW

56.7%
AERIAL DUELS WON
A LEAGUE HUGH

14
DRAWS
A JOINT-LEAGUE HIGH

LIVERPOOL

2023 POSITION: 5TH

TOP SCORER: MOHAMED SALAH (19)
TOP ASSISTS: MOHAMED SALAH (12)
MOST MINUTES: ALISSON (3330)

9
GOALS SCORED
IN ONE GAME
A LEAGUE HIGH

61%
POSSESSION

799
CROSSES - A LEAGUE HIGH

There was a time last season when it felt like Jurgen Klopp was skating on thin ice, as managers around him were being sacked left, right and centre! The man himself even admitted that his excellent track record was the only thing keeping him in a job. But, in typical fighting fashion, The Reds ended the season as the league's on form club and salvaged a spot in the Europa League. They were dreaming of much bigger things at the start the season, but after their awful start it was a good achivement. In 2023-24 they'll be focused on getting back into the Champions League, although their new-look midfield and forwards will need time to reach the levels of the 2018-19 and 2019-20 performances.

15.9
SHOTS PER
GAME

84%
PASS SUCCESS RATE

Stats from 2022-23 season

17 SET-PIECE GOALS
A LEAGUE HIGH

BRIGHTON

2023 POSITION: 6TH

TOP SCORER: ALEXIS MAC ALLISTER (10)
TOP ASSISTS: PASCAL GROSS (8)
MOST MINUTES: PASCAL GROSS (3246)

232
SHOTS ON TARGET
A LEAGUE HIGH

16.1
SHOTS PER GAME
A LEAGUE HIGH

86%
PASS SUCCESS RATE

Losing Graham Potter to Chelsea was like a dagger in the hearts of most Brighton fans, but in the end it turned out to be a great thing to happen to the club. Roberto De Zerbi didn't just continue where Potter left off, he managed to get even more out of the squad in 2022-23. With their quick-passing style of play, they are easily one of the best teams to watch in the Premier League and regularly boast higher possession stats than their opponents, even when playing against teams with far bigger budgets than them, like Man. United, Chelsea and Tottenham. The key to their continuing success has been their incredible recruitment - they sign unknown gems for next to nothing and transform them into Premier League stars!

44%
ROBERTO
DE ZERBI
WIN RATE

3,520
LEWIS DUNK TOUCHES
A LEAGUE HIGH

6 OWN GOALS
A LEAGUE HIGH

27

ASTON VILLA

2023 POSITION: 7TH

TOP SCORER: OLLIE WATKINS (15)
TOP ASSISTS: JACOB RAMSEY (7)
MOST MINUTES: EZRI KONSA (3323)

11.3
SHOTS PER GAME

21
TIMES HIT WOODWORK

80
YELLOW CARDS

60%
UNAI EMERY
WIN RATE

498
FOULED
A LEAGUE HIGH

5 COUNTER ATTACK
GOALS

When Unai Emery was announced as Aston Villa manager in November 2022, he said that he had two objectives: to win a trophy at the club and to play in a European competition with them! After securing Europa Conference League football thanks to their impressive ten-game unbeaten run between February and April 2023, he's already achieved half of his targets, so now he's got his eyes on part two: silverware. He's already proven that he's more than capable of pulling it off - no manager has lifted more Europa League titles in history, while he also led Arsenal to the final of the tournament in 2019. Can he guide The Villans to the Europa Conference League trophy and their first major piece of silverware since 1996?

Stats from 2022-23 season

TOTTENHAM

2023 POSITION: 8TH

TOP SCORER: HARRY KANE (30)
TOP ASSISTS: IVAN PERISIC (8)
MOST MINUTES: HARRY KANE (3408)

5
KANE GOALS
ASSISTED
BY DEJAN
KULUSEVSKI

16
SET-PIECE GOALS

6
DRAWS

The 2022-23 season was frustrating, to say the least, for Tottenham fans. They went from losing just one of their first ten games – to North London rivals Arsenal – and ending the calendar year nestled in the top four, to sacking two managers in the space of a month and finishing without any European football for the first time in a decade. There's clearly some real quality in the Spurs squad and they should definitely be targeting a return to the Champions League, but a lot will depend on how they manage a period of transition, with some of their biggest stars either getting old or moving on. New manager Ange Postecoglou has a huge job on his hands!

43%
GOALS SCORED
BY HARRY KANE

5.2
SHOTS ON TARGET
PER GAME

63 GOALS
CONCEDED

29

BRENTFORD

2023 POSITION: 9TH

TOP SCORER: IVAN TONEY (20)
TOP ASSISTS: BRYAN MBEUMO (8)
MOST MINUTES: DAVID RAYA (3420)

132
BEN MEE AERIALS WON
A LEAGUE HIGH

214
ETHAN PINNOCK CLEARANCES
A LEAGUE HIGH

154
DAVID RAYA SAVES
A LEAGUE HIGH

Brentford boss Thomas Frank well and truly deserved his nomination for the Premier League Manager of the Year prize in 2023. Many pundits predicted The Bees to be near the relegation zone last term, so to finish above their west London rivals Chelsea is an incredible achievement - especially when you consider that The Bees' most-used starting XI last season cost less than Kalidou Koulibaly alone! With one of the smallest budgets in the league it could be tricky to keep their success going next season, while Frank will always be linked with the Premier League's top clubs. But the Brentford Community Stadium will still be one of the toughest places to go in the league!

668
AERIALS WON
A LEAGUE HIGH

2,312
LONG BALLS
A LEAGUE HIGH

14 DRAWS
A JOINT-LEAGUE HIGH

Stats from 2022-23 season

30

FULHAM

2023 POSITION: 10TH

TOP SCORER: ALEKSANDR MITROVIC (14)
TOP ASSISTS: ANDREAS PEREIRA (6)
MOST MINUTES: BERND LENO (3240)

15
HEADED GOALS
A JOINT-LEAGUE HIGH

27.9
AVERAGE AGE
OF SQUAD
A JOINT-LEAGUE HIGH

80
YELLOW CARDS

Like Brentford and Thomas Frank, Fulham and Marco Silva were hugh overachievers in 2022-23! By late February 2023, The Cottagers were well in the race for one of England's European spots, until a run of just two wins in ten games consigned them to a mid-table finish. It's perhaps no surprise that their run of poor form coincided with the loss of star striker Aleksandar Mitrovic, who was handed an eight-game ban for inexplicably pushing referee Chris Kavanagh in the team's FA Cup loss against Man. United. This season they'll have Raul Jimenez leading the line instead, and they'll need the Mexico striker to stay fit and firing to improve on last year.

144
BERND LENO SAVES

147
JOAO PALHINHA TACKLES
A LEAGUE HIGH

14 JOAO PALHINHA
YELLOW CARDS

CRYSTAL PALACE

2023 POSITION: 11TH

TOP SCORER: EBERECHI EZE (10)
TOP ASSISTS: MICHAEL OLISE (11)
MOST MINUTES: MARC GUEHI (3330)

5
COUNTER-ATTACK GOALS

5
MICHAEL OLISE ASSISTS FOR EZE

26
POINTS AFTER FALLING BEHIND
A LEAGUE HIGH

Even when Crystal Palace went on their mid-season wobble at the start of 2023, failing to win any of their first 12 games of the year, they still didn't fall below 12th in the table! Their poor form cost Patrick Vieira his job, with Roy Hodgson coming out of retirement to take charge of The Eagles for the second time. The veteran boss enjoyed steering Palace to safety so much that he decided to stay for another season, extending his record as the PL's oldest-ever manager! He'll need to build a new-look side after club legend Wilf Zaha left for Galatasaray, but with the likes of Jefferson Lerma, Marc Guehi and Eberechi Eze, there's plenty of talent to work with!

71
EBERECHI EZE
SUCCESSFUL DRIBBLES
A LEAGUE HIGH

50%
ROY HODGSON WIN RATE

3 RED CARDS

CHELSEA

2023 POSITION: 12TH

TOP SCORER: KAI HAVERTZ (7)
TOP ASSISTS: HAKIM ZIYECH & RAHEEM STERLING (3)
MOST MINUTES: KAI HAVERTZ (2580)

6
LAST-MAN TACKLES
A JOINT-LEAGUE HIGH

14
KAI HAVERTZ
BIG CHANCES
MISSED

32
PLAYERS USED

Last season can only be described as a nightmare for Chelsea fans. Despite spending over £500 million on the most expensive squad in Europe, and hiring one of the league's most exciting young managers in Graham Potter, they quite literally couldn't buy a win. The managerial merry-go-round that saw Frank Lampard briefly take over finally stopped at Mauricio Pochettino, the ex-Tottenham manager who famously guided Spurs to the final of the Champions League. His experience of working at another European giant in PSG, managing the likes of Kylian Mbappe, Lionel Messi and Neymar, should be just what this Blues squad needs to rediscover their mojo!

833
TOTAL DRIBBLES
A LEAGUE HIGH

66%
GOALS FROM
OPEN PLAY

1 GAME WON UNDER
FRANK LAMPARD

WOLVES

2023 POSITION: 13TH

TOP SCORER: DANIEL PODENCE & RUBEN NEVES (6)
TOP ASSISTS: JOAO MOUTINHO (2)
MOST MINUTES: MAX KILMAN (3308)

31
GOALS SCORED
A LEAGUE LOW

28
FOREIGN
PLAYERS USED
A LEAGUE HIGH

81%
PASS SUCCESS RATE

Christmas 2022 was supposed to be a time of celebration, but things were looking bleak for Wolves as they sat rock-bottom of the Premier League table with just two wins from their first 15 matches. However, their newly appointed manager Julen Lopetegui provided a Christmas miracle to steer the West Midlands team towards safety, as they became just the fourth side in Premier League history to have escaped relegation after being bottom on Christmas Day. The experienced gaffer's exit from Molineux was confirmed just three days before the 2023-24 Premier League season started, with former Bournemouth boss Gary O'Neil taking over ahead of the club's sixth straight season in the top tier!

84
YELLOW CARDS
A JOINT-LEAGUE HIGH

375
SUCCESSFUL DRIBBLES
A JOINT-LEAGUE HIGH

6 RED CARDS
A LEAGUE HIGH

Stats from 2022-23 season

34

WEST HAM

2023 POSITION: 14TH

TOP SCORER: JARROD BOWEN & SAID BENRAHMA (6)
TOP ASSISTS: JARROD BOWEN (5)
MOST MINUTES: DECLAN RICE (3272)

27.9
AVERAGE AGE
OF SQUAD
A JOINT-LEAGUE HIGH

25
PLAYERS USED

16
TACKLES PER GAME

The Hammers' hopes of establishing themselves as the "best of the rest" took a hit last season as they spent most of the campaign near the drop zone. Some positive results in key moments meant they were relatively stress-free in the final weeks of the 2022-23 season, and they took that form into Europe. The Europa Conference League was the club's first major trophy in 43 years, and means that they'll play in the Europa League in 2023-24. They'll have to do it without inspirational captain Declan Rice, who joined Arsenal for £105 million, but if David Moyes can rebuild a new-look team with a new-look midfield, The Hammers have a strong chance of another good run in Europe and a return to the top half of the Prem!

768
CROSSES

43
YELLOW CARDS
A JOINT-LEAGUE LOW

0 REDS CARDS
A JOINT-LEAGUE LOW

BOURNEMOUTH

2023 POSITION: 15TH

TOP SCORER: PHILIP BILLING (7)
TOP ASSISTS: DOMINIC SOLANKE (7)
MOST MINUTES: JEFFERSON LERMA (3256)

38
OFFSIDES
A LEAGUE LOW

527
HEADED CLEARANCES
A LEAGUE HIGH

6
LAST-MAN TACKLES
A JOINT-LEAGUE HIGH

Bournemouth fans must have been worried that their 9-0 loss to Liverpool at the start of last season was going to be a sign of things to come but, thankfully for them, they improved a lot after Gary O'Neil replaced Scott Parker as manager. They picked up key victories against many of the teams around them, including Nottingham Forest, Leeds, Southampton, Everton and Leicester, but those wins weren't enough to keep O'Neill in the job. The club took a gamble by changing their manager again, but have poached one of Europe's most exciting coaching talents. Andoni Iraola helped Rayo Vallecano punch above their weight in La Liga last season - now he needs to do the same with The Cherries!

0
OWN GOALS
A JOINT-LEAGUE LOW

971
CLEARANCES
A LEAGUE HIGH

527
HEADED CLEARANCES
A LEAGUE HIGH

0 PENALTIES SCORED
A LEAGUE LOW

Stats from 2022-23 season

36

NOTTINGHAM FOREST

2023 POSITION: 16TH

TOP SCORER: TAIWO AWONIYI (10)
TOP ASSISTS: MORGAN GIBBS-WHITE (8)
MOST MINUTES: MORGAN GIBBS-WHITE (2978)

2
GOALS SCORED FROM
OUTSIDE THE BOX
A LEAGUE LOW

2
DEAN HENDERSON PENALTIES SAVED
A JOINT-LEAGUE HIGH

128
CORNERS TAKEN
A LEAGUE LOW

30
INCOMING
TRANSFERS
COMPLETED
A LEAGUE HIGH

12,091
PASSES
A LEAGUE LOW

Nottingham Forest made 21 signings in the summer of 2022, breaking the English record for the most arrivals in one transfer window. They also set a new club transfer record by bringing in midfielder Morgan Gibbs-White from Wolves for a reported initial fee of £25 million. It was always going to be tough for Steve Cooper to make all the new signings gel - and quickly - but he helped the club achieve their goal of staying up by bagging 11 points from their last six games, including impressive wins over Brighton, Southampton and Arsenal. The 2023-24 campaign will be the first time since the mid-1990s that the former two-time European Cup winners have spent back-to-back seasons in the top flight!

1,763 BACKWARD PASSES
A LEAGUE LOW

37

EVERTON

2023 POSITION: 17TH

TOP SCORER: DWIGHT MCNEIL (7)
TOP ASSISTS: ALEX IWOBI (7)
MOST MINUTES: JAMES TARKOWSKI (3420)

124
JORDAN PICKFORD
SAVES

180
SHOTS BLOCKED
A LEAGUE HIGH

1
PLAYER WITH 10+ GOALS
& ASSISTS COMBINED

The emotions at the final whistle of Everton's last game of the 2022-23 season, a 1-0 win over Bournemouth to secure their Premier League status, ranged from relief to rage as Toffees fans vented over how they had once again found themselves in such a dangerous position. The Merseyside club have spent 121 seasons in the English top flight, more than any other team, but that record looked seriously under threat until Abdoulaye Doucoure's second-half strike sealed the win against The Cherries that kept them up. The men in blue would love a season without a relegation battle to worry about and, with Sean Dyche in charge, they have a man who knows all about building teams that are tough to beat.

28%
SEAN DYCHE'S
WIN RATE

10
COUNTER-ATTACK
GOALS CONCEDED
A LEAGUE HIGH

60 LONG BALLS
PER GAME

Stats from 2022-23 season

BURNLEY

2023 POSITION: 1ST CHAMPIONSHIP

TOP SCORER: NATHAN TELLA (17)
TOP ASSISTS: JOSH BROWNHILL (8)
MOST MINUTES: JOSH CULLEN (3844)

87
GOALS SCORED
A LEAGUE HIGH

CHAMPIONS

101
TOTAL POINTS

47
AWAY POINTS
A LEAGUE HIGH

64.6%
AVERAGE
POSSESSION
A LEAGUE HIGH

35
GOALS CONCEDED
A LEAGUE LOW

In the six seasons that Burnley spent in the Premier League before being relegated in 2021-22, they built a reputation for playing aggressive, long-ball football. But now, under former Man. City captain Vincent Kompany, they're a completely different side. Last season they dominated the Championship using the attacking, passing tactics that Kompany played under Pep Guardiola at Man. City, bossing more possession than any other team in the league. Using that style in the Prem will be much harder, so keeping them up will be the biggest challenge of Kompany's career in football, but he's committed to the job after signing a new contract to keep him at Turf Moor until 2028.

1 HOME DEFEAT
A LEAGUE LOW

SHEFFIELD UNITED

2023 POSITION: 2ND CHAMPIONSHIP

TOP SCORER: ILIMAN NDIAYE (14)
TOP ASSISTS: ILIMAN NDIAYE (10)
MOST MINUTES: JOHN EGAN (3955)

18
TACKLES PER GAME

112
ILIMAN NDIAYE
COMPLETED DRIBBLES

22
GOALS SCORED
FROM SET-PIECES

As well as finishing second in the Championship last season, Sheffield United also proved their Premier League credentials in the FA Cup, first by beating Tottenham at home in the fifth round and then taking on Man. City in the semi-final at Wembley! They managed to keep out the eventual winners until the stroke of half-time before being undone by a Riyad Mahrez hat-trick, but they proved they will be a tough team to face in the top flight. Manager Paul Heckingbottom was the interim boss at the end of The Blades' last Prem campaign in 2020-21, but he returns to the top tier with loads more experience and a strong determination to avoid relegation this time!

229
SHOTS
ON TARGET
A LEAGUE HIGH

102
YELLOW CARDS

0 GOALS SCORED FROM PENALTIES
A JOINT-LEAGUE LOW

Stats from 2022-23 season

40

LUTON

2023 POSITION: 3RD CHAMPIONSHIP

TOP SCORER: CARLTON MORRIS (20)
TOP ASSISTS: CARLTON MORRIS (7)
MOST MINUTES: ETHAN HORVATH (4261)

24
AERIAL DUELS
WON PER GAME

95
ETHAN
HORVATH
SAVES

193
TOM LOCKYER
CLEARANCES

Luton's Hollywood rise from non-league football to the Premier League was complete in 2023 when they beat Coventry 6-5 on penalties to win the Championship play-off final at Wembley! The last time they were a top-flight side was way back in 1992, just before the Premier League began. They went down and kept on going, spending four seasons in the National League between 2010 and 2014, so their comeback has been quite incredible! Whatever happens, 2024 will be the eighth year in a row that The Hatters have improved their league position, and nobody will enjoy visiting their small, old-fashioned ground at Kenilworth Road. Can the fairytale continue?

12.4
FOULS PER GAME
A LEAGUE HIGH

43%
GOALS SCORED BY
CARLTON MORRIS

16 GOALS SCORED
FROM SET-PIECES

Stats from 2022-23 season

41

WORD**FIT**

BERGKAMP

Aguero	Ferdinand	Keane	Le Saux	Okocha	Vidic
Bergkamp	Ferguson	Klinsmann	Le Tissier	Schmeichel	Viduka
Cole	Gerrard	King	Makelele	Shearer	Vieira
Di Canio	Ginola	Kompany	McManaman	Terry	Yorke
Drogba	Henry	Lampard	Modric	Toure	Zola

ACTION REPLAY

1 Who started the game up front for Arsenal – Gabriel Jesus or Eddie Nketiah?

2 Name the Man. City defender who scored City's second on the stroke of half-time!

3 How long did it take Kevin De Bruyne to open the deadlock – three minutes, five minutes or seven minutes?

4 True or False? It was Guardiola's biggest-ever win over Arsenal!

5 How many yellow cards were there in total – four, six or eight?

6 Which young talent came on for City in the 80th minute – Cole Palmer, Julian Alvarez or Sergio Gomez?

7 True or False? Erling Haaland scored the game's last goal in the 95th minute!

8 Who got the assist for Rob Holding's late consolation – Leandro Trossard, Bukayo Saka or Gabriel Martinelli?

9 Which team had more possession of the ball – Arsenal or Man. City?

HOW MUCH CAN YOU REMEMBER FROM MAN. CITY'S CRUCIAL 4-1 WIN OVER ARSENAL LAST SEASON?

ANSWERS ON PAGE 60

PREMIER LEAGUE
MANAGERS OF THE MONTH

THERE WERE ONLY FOUR DIFFERENT WINNERS OF THE PREMIER LEAGUE MANAGER OF THE MONTH IN 2022-23, WITH ARSENAL'S MIKEL ARTETA CLAIMING THE PRIZE MORE THAN ANYONE ELSE. HOWEVER, NONE OF THEM WENT ON TO WIN THE MANAGER OF THE YEAR AWARD.

AUGUST
MIKEL ARTETA
ARSENAL

WINS: 5
DRAWS: 0
DEFEATS: 0
GOALS FOR: 13
GOALS AGAINST: 4
BEST RESULT:
BOURNEMOUTH 0-3 ARSENAL

OCTOBER
EDDIE HOWE
NEWCASTLE

WINS: 5
DRAWS: 1
DEFEATS: 0
GOALS FOR: 16
GOALS AGAINST: 3
BEST RESULT:
NEWCASTLE 5-1 BRENTFORD

SEPTEMBER
ERIK TEN HAG
MAN. UNITED

WINS: 2
DRAWS: 0
DEFEATS: 0
GOALS FOR: 4
GOALS AGAINST: 1
BEST RESULT:
MAN. UNITED 3-1 ARSENAL

JANUARY
MIKEL ARTETA
ARSENAL

WINS: 2
DRAWS: 1
DEFEATS: 0
GOALS FOR: 5
GOALS AGAINST: 3
BEST RESULT:
TOTTENHAM 0-2 ARSENAL

NOVEMBER & DECEMBER
MIKEL ARTETA
ARSENAL

WINS: 4
DRAWS: 0
DEFEATS: 0
GOALS FOR: 10
GOALS AGAINST: 3
BEST RESULT:
BRIGHTON 2-4 ARSENAL

FEBRUARY
ERIK TEN HAG
MAN. UNITED

WINS: 3
DRAWS: 1
DEFEATS: 0
GOALS FOR: 9
GOALS AGAINST: 3
BEST RESULT:
MAN. UNITED 3-0 LEICESTER

MARCH
MIKEL ARTETA
ARSENAL

WINS: 4
DRAWS: 0
DEFEATS: 0
GOALS FOR: 14
GOALS AGAINST: 3
BEST RESULT:
ARSENAL 4-0 EVERTON

APRIL
UNAI EMERY
ASTON VILLA

WINS: 5
DRAWS: 1
DEFEATS: 1
GOALS FOR: 11
GOALS AGAINST: 3
BEST RESULT:
ASTON VILLA 3-0 NEWCASTLE

PREMIER

MANAGER
OF THE YEAR

PEP GUARDIOLA

Man. City gaffer Pep Guardiola was named the Premier League's Manager of the Year for a fourth time, having also won the prize in three previous title-winning campaigns: 2017-18, 2018-19 and 2020-21! He's now in second place for the most Manager of the Season awards, moving above Arsene Wenger and Jose Mourinho, with only former Man. United manager Sir Alex Ferguson ahead of him. It'll take him a long time to catch up with the legendary Scot's record of 11 though!

Pep did match another of Ferguson's records at least, winning his third consecutive PL title. Since the Spanish coach arrived at Man. City in 2016, he has lifted the Premier League trophy five times, with last season's battle with Mikel Arteta and Arsenal one of his toughest title tussles yet.

Guardiola made it a hat-trick of individual honours for Man. City in 2022-23 after Erling Haaland collected both the Player and Young Player of the Season awards!

LEAGUE

"I'M DELIGHTED, IT'S AN INCREDIBLE HONOUR. I PROMISE YOU NEXT SEASON WE WILL BE THERE TO FIGHT AGAIN TO DIGNIFY THIS LEAGUE AS MUCH AS POSSIBLE."

MANAGERS SHORTLISTED FOR THE AWARD:

PEP GUARDIOLA
MAN. CITY

UNAI EMERY
ASTON VILLA

EDDIE HOWE
NEWCASTLE

MIKEL ARTETA
ARSENAL

ROBERTO DE ZERBI
BRIGHTON

MARCO SILVA
FULHAM

GOLDEN GLOVE WINNER

Man. United's David De Gea won the 2022-23 Golden Glove after keeping 17 clean sheets; three more than Alisson, Nick Pope and Aaron Ramsdale in joint second. It's the second time the Spanish shot-stopper has claimed the award, winning in 2017-18 with 18 clean sheets.

TEAM OF THE SEASON

Check out the EA Sports' FIFA 23 Premier League Team of the Season, as voted for by the community. There was no room for the likes of Heung-min Son, Bukayo Saka or Gabriel Martinelli.

AARON RAMSDALE
ARSENAL

KIERAN TRIPPIER
NEWCASTLE

WILLIAM SALIBA
ARSENAL

RUBEN DIAS
MAN. CITY

OLEKSANDR ZINCHENKO
ARSENAL

CASEMIRO
MAN. UNITED

MARTIN ODEGAARD
ARSENAL

KEVIN DE BRUYNE
MAN. CITY

MOHAMED SALAH
LIVERPOOL

ERLING HAALAND
MAN. CITY

MARCUS RASHFORD
MAN. UNITED

MY 2023-24
PREMIER LEAGUE TEAM OF THE SEASON

Who do you think will be in the Premier League Team of the Season for 2023-24? Fill in your selections and when the team is announced at the end of the campaign, compare with the team you predicted.

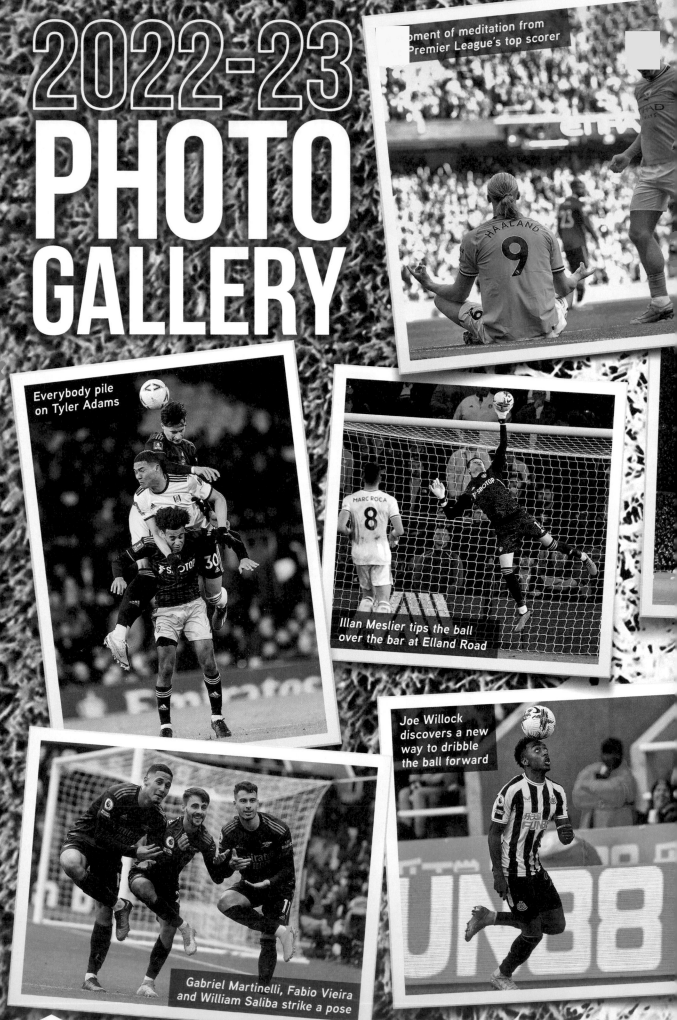

2022-23 PHOTO GALLERY

Moment of meditation from Premier League's top scorer

Everybody pile on Tyler Adams

Illan Meslier tips the ball over the bar at Elland Road

Joe Willock discovers a new way to dribble the ball forward

Gabriel Martinelli, Fabio Vieira and William Saliba strike a pose

Mohamed Salah celebrates in front of a poster of himself

Harry Maguire tussles with then-Brighton winger Leandro Trossard

HARRY KANE
TOTTENHAM HOTSPUR
ALL-TIME RECORD GOALSCORER

The moment Harry Kane became Tottenham's record goalscorer

Ivan Toney goes for a scissor kick against Aston Villa

Leicester's Patson Daka produces an acrobatic celebration

A Chelsea fan kisses Mateo Kovacic on the arm after receiving his shirt

Jesse Lingard was placed on cone duty at the Forest Ground

BRAINBUSTER

HOW'S YOUR PREMIER LEAGUE GENERAL KNOWLEDGE? TAKE THIS TEST TO FIND OUT...

1 How many teams were there in the first-ever PL campaign back in 1992-93 – 18, 20 or 22?

2 Which team wasn't one of the PL's founding members – Bristol City, Middlesbrough or Oldham?

3 Name the Premier League club who won four out of the first five league titles!

4 True or False? In the 2010s, Tottenham finished in the top six more times than Liverpool!

5 Who lifted the trophy as Leicester captain in the historic 2015-16 season?

6 Name the four London clubs who have never been relegated from the Premier League!

7 Who was the first Welsh team to appear in the Premier League – Cardiff or Swansea?

8 How many Premier League clubs has Frank Lampard managed in his career?

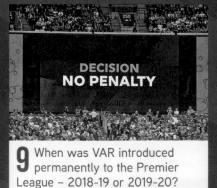

9 When was VAR introduced permanently to the Premier League – 2018-19 or 2019-20?

10 Name the global sports brand that makes the footballs for the Premier League!

1. ....

2. ....

3. ....

4. ....

5. ....

6. ....

....

7. ....

8. ....

9. ....

10. ....

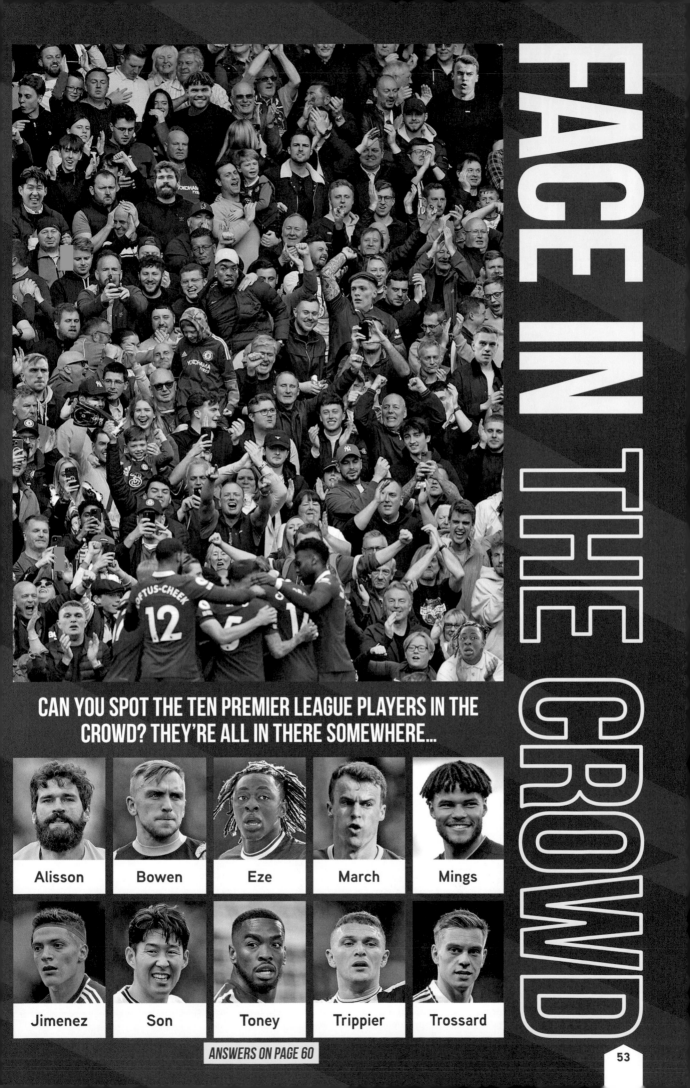

FACE IN THE CROWD

CAN YOU SPOT THE TEN PREMIER LEAGUE PLAYERS IN THE CROWD? THEY'RE ALL IN THERE SOMEWHERE...

Alisson	Bowen	Eze	March	Mings

Jimenez	Son	Toney	Trippier	Trossard

ANSWERS ON PAGE 60

PREMIER LEAGUE
You Tube CLIPS

HERE ARE SOME OF THE BEST YOUTUBE CLIPS ON THE OFFICIAL PREMIER LEAGUE CHANNEL

PREMIER LEAGUE QR CODES EXPLAINED

This is a QR code – just scan it with your phone or tablet to watch each video clip on YouTube. Here's how to do it:

Open the camera on your phone or tablet and hold it over the QR code. Click on the link and you'll be sent to the clip. Easy!

▶ ⏭ 1:35 / 8:12

▶ NO-LOOK COMPILATION

There aren't many cooler things in footy than no-look goals and passes, and this video counts down ten of the best from the likes of Roberto Firmino, Phil Foden and Mesut Ozil! You'll be trying to recreate them after watching this...

▶ INTERNATIONAL NET-BUSTERS!

The Prem has been home to players from all over the world, so this video presents an amazing goal from every nation to have featured in the league – from Albania, to Iran and Peru!

▶ ⏭ 1:35 / 8:12   HD 🔊 ⛶

▶ ▶| 1:35 / 8:12　　　　HD ◀》 []

▶ GREATEST-EVER RIVALRY!

Arsenal and Man. United have won 16 Prem titles between them and all of them came under just two managers. This video is all about the rivalry between the legends Arsene Wenger and Sir Alex Ferguson!

▶ ▶| 1:35 / 8:12　　　　HD ◀》 []

▶ THE COMPLETE STRIKER!

Former Chelsea striker Didier Drogba is one of the best forwards the Premier League has ever witnessed, and this five-minute highlights reel, featuring his best goals, assists and skills, is all the proof that you need!

[center image of a football pitch with players]

▶ SOLO STUNNERS!

This compilation of the best solo goals scored in the Premier League features some truly iconic goals, like Heung-min Son's Puskas winner and Hatem Ben Arfa's incredible run and finish against Bolton!

▶ ▶| 1:35 / 8:12　　　　HD ◀》 []

▶ ▶| 1:35 / 8:12　　　　HD ◀》 []

▶ GAME OF THE CENTURY!

As the 1995-96 Premier League drew to a close, Kevin Keegan's Newcastle desperately needed a win away at Anfield. Here's the story of how this title-decider became known as the Game of the Century...

▶ ▶| 1:35 / 8:12　　　　HD ◀》 []

▶ KANE'S CHALLENGE!

After netting his 200th Premier League goal in 2023, Harry Kane tried to recreate some of the best finishes from his career - plus with a little bit of help from the league's all-time record goalscorer, Alan Shearer!

PREMIER LEAGUE HALL OF FAME

CHECK OUT FIVE OF THE 2023 INDUCTEES INTO THE PREMIER LEAGUE HALL OF FAME...

RIO FERDINAND

Rio Ferdinand emerged onto the scene at West Ham as a 17-year-old wonderkid, before Leeds made him the most expensive defender in the world in 2000. Man. United then broke the British transfer record to sign him two seasons later, where he would become a Premier League legend, lifting the title six times!

DID YOU KNOW?
The Premier League Hall of Fame was introduced in 2021 to celebrate the legends of the league!

ARSENE WENGER

Despite arriving at the club as a relatively unknown figure in the game, it didn't take long for Arsene Wenger to make his mark on North London. During his reign, Arsenal became known for their possession-based, free-flowing footy, which led them to three Premier League titles, including the historic "Invincibles" unbeaten season of 2003-04!

SIR ALEX FERGUSON

The most successful manager in British football history, Sir Alex Ferguson lifted 13 Premier League titles while in charge of Man. United, ending their 26-year wait for a top-flight title in the first Premier League season of 1992-93. He's also the only manager to win the Manager of the Year award as many as 11 times!

HALL OF FAME!

HERE ARE THE OTHER PLAYERS ALREADY IN THE HALL OF FAME!

Sergio Aguero

David Beckham

Dennis Bergkamp

Eric Cantona

Didier Drogba

Steven Gerrard

Thierry Henry

Roy Keane

Vincent Kompany

Frank Lampard

Wayne Rooney

Peter Schmeichel

Paul Scholes

Alan Shearer

Patrick Vieira

Ian Wright

TONY ADAMS

Centre-back Tony Adams was Arsenal through and through, spending his entire career at the club and captaining them to two Premier League titles in 1997-98 and 2001-02. Although he was a tough centre-back, he sealed the 1998 title with a sweetly struck left-footed volley against Everton near the end of the season!

PETR CECH

In his debut season at Chelsea in 2004-05, Petr Cech registered 24 clean sheets, which remains a Premier League record for the most in a single campaign. He won four league titles and three Golden Gloves in 11 seasons at Stamford Bridge, before switching to Arsenal and adding another Golden Glove to his collection in 2015-16!

THE NEW BOYS!

DID YOU KNOW?

His transfer to Newcastle made him the most expensive Italian player of all time!

SANDRO TONALI

Newcastle marked their return to Champions League football by signing a star who played in the semi-finals of last season's competition. The defensive midfielder played more minutes than any other player in Milan's run to the last four, and also played a crucial role in their 2021-22 Serie A title win. The 23-year-old arrives in England with 14 Italy caps and with a big future in the game!

CHRISTOPHER NKUNKU

The PSG academy graduate won three Ligue 1 titles with the French giants before moving to RB Leipzig in 2019. He impressed in the Bundesliga straight away, with 13 assists in his debut campaign, then helped the team finish second in his second season, before scoring 20 goals for the first time in 2021-22. He was named Player of the Season and followed that up by sharing the 2022-23 Golden Boot with 16 goals!

DID YOU KNOW?

Nkunku once bagged four assists in the space of just 30 minutes in a Bundesliga game against Schalke back in 2020!

58

DID YOU KNOW?

He became Liverpool's third-most expensive signing of all time, and the third Hungarian to play for the club!

DOMINIK SZOBOSZLAI

Liverpool triggered the Hungary captain's £60 million release clause to make him their second major signing of the 2023 summer window after Alexis Mac Allister from Brighton! Szoboszlai's favourite position is number ten, but he's also played deeper in centre-mid or on the wing for his former sides RB Leipzig and Salzburg. He's not afraid of taking on a challenge, as he showed by choosing The Reds' famous no.8 jersey, which was previously worn by club legend Steven Gerrard!

JURRIEN TIMBER

The versatile Dutch defender, who can play as a centre-back or right-back, was wanted by Man. United in the summer of 2022, but ended up staying at Ajax for another season. By joining Arsenal in 2023, he became the latest in a long line of players to leave the Dutch giants for the Premier League, following the likes of Antony, Lisandro Martinez, Davinson Sanchez and Hakim Ziyech!

DID YOU KNOW?

He made more successful passes and forward passes than any other player in the Eredivisie in 2022-23!

LEAVING LEGENDS!

THE PREMIER LEAGUE SAID GOODBYE TO SOME LEGENDS IN 2023...

N'Golo Kante

The ex-Leicester and Chelsea midfielder became the first outfield player to win consecutive PL titles with two different clubs!

Roberto Firmino

The Liverpool cult hero was part of a formidable attacking trio with Sadio Mane and Mohamed Salah!

Harry Kane

The England captain joined Bayern Munich, calling time on his record-breaking spell at boyhood club Tottenham!

Ilkay Gundogan

Gundo will be remembered as the first player to lift the Champions League trophy as a Man. City captain!

Cesar Azpilicueta

No other non-English player has made more appearances for Chelsea - plus, he led them to the Champions League as captain in 2021!

QUIZ ANSWERS

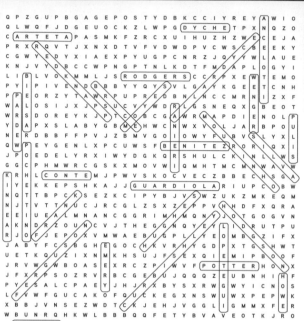

QUIZ ONE

Wordsearch: See right.
Spot The Difference: See above.

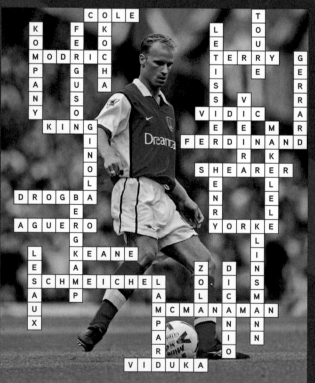

QUIZ TWO

Wordfit: See above.
Action Replay: 1. Gabriel Jesus; 2. John Stones;
3. Seven minutes; 4. False, he beat Arsenal
5-0 in 2021; 5. Four; 6. Julian Alvarez;
7. True; 8. Leandro Trossard; 9. Man. City.

QUIZ THREE

Brainbuster: 1. 22; 2. Bristol City; 3. Man. United;
4. True; 5. Wes Morgan; 6. Arsenal, Chelsea,
Tottenham and Brentford; 7. Swansea; 8. Two
(Chelsea and Everton); 9. 2019-20; 10. Nike.
Face in the Crowd: See above.

PREMIER LLAGUE RECORDS

WE DELVE INTO THE PREMIER LEAGUE RECORD BOOKS...

APPEARANCES

Former Aston Villa, Man. City, Everton and West Brom midfielder **Gareth Barry** holds the record for the most appearances in the Premier League, racking up 653 throughout his 22-year career!

GOALS

With 260 goals, **Alan Shearer** sits top of the Premier League scoring charts after scoring for fun in the Premier League at Blackburn and Newcastle. He was the league's top scorer as Rovers lifted the title in the 1994-95 season!

ASSISTS

A rare one-club player, **Ryan Giggs** spent his entire senior career at Man. United and retired with a record 162 assists. **Kevin De Bruyne** and **Thierry Henry** share the record for the most assists (20) in a single season!

CLEAN SHEETS

The only goalkeeper to reach 200 Premier League clean sheets is **Petr Cech**, who ended with 202! The Czech Republic hero played a combined 443 league matches for London rivals Chelsea and Arsenal, and won four Golden Gloves!

COACH WINS

The only Premier League manager to win over 500 games is **Sir Alex Ferguson**, boasting an incredible 65% win rate during his 528 PL games in charge of Man. United. Only **Arsene Wenger** has taken charge of more Prem games!

YOUNGEST PLAYER

By coming on as a stoppage-time substitute against Brentford in September 2022, Arsenal wonderkid **Ethan Nwaneri** became the youngest player in Premier League history, aged 15 years and 181 days!